My Front Porch

AN INVITATION TO THE CHARM AND TRADITION

Alda Ellis

PAINTINGS BY
Sandy Lynam Clough

HARVEST HOUSE PUBLISHERS
Eugene, Oregon

My Front Porch

Copyright © 1999 Alda Ellis
Published by Harvest House Publishers
Eugene, Oregon 97402

Library of Congress Cataloging-in-Publication Data
    Ellis, Alda, 1952-
      My front porch / Alda Ellis.
        p.   cm.
      ISBN 0-7369-0010-1
      1. Hospitality—United States.   2. Entertaining—United States-
    3. Porches—Decoration—United States.   4. Porches—Social aspects-
-United States.   I. Title.
    BJ2021.E45 1999
    395.3—dc21   98-31112
                                     CIP

All works of art reproduced in this book are copyrighted by Sandy Lynam Clough and may not be reproduced without the artist's permission. For information regarding art prints featured in this book, please contact:

    Sandy Clough Studios
    25 Trail Road
    Marietta, GA 30064
    (800) 447-8409

Design and production by Garborg Design Works, Minneapolis, Minnesota

Scripture quotations are from the Holy Bible, New International Version®. Copyright © 1973, 1978, 1984 by the International Bible Society. Used by permission of Zondervan Publishing House; the New American Standard Bible, © 1960, 1962, 1963, 1968, 1971, 1972, 1973, 1975, 1977, 1995 by The Lockman Foundation. Used by permission; The Living Bible, © 1971 owned by assignment by Illinois Regional Bank N.A. (as trustee). Used by permission of Tyndale House Publishers, Inc., Wheaton, Illinois 60189. All rights reserved.

Printed in the United States of America.

99 00 01 02 03 04 05 06 07 08 / IP / 10 9 8 7 6 5 4 3 2

C O N T E N T S

The Welcoming Spirit of the Front Porch

When I was a child, my grandmother used to tell me that a front porch was a postcard that gave a glimpse of who lived inside the house. Back then, I was not quite sure what Grandmother meant. But now, years later, I see the front porch as my grandmother did.

To me, a cheerful porch is a sure sign of a welcoming and open heart. By looking at the front porch, I can catch a glimpse of the personality of the home long before its owner opens the door. I've seen grand porches that welcome the approaching guest with charming decorator touches and architectural detailing, and I've seen tiny little porches that smile with simple yet sincere touches. Some porches are large enough to host big family get-togethers, while others hold just one or two quite cozily. Some porches aren't even porches at all—a cement stoop dressed with a creative welcome mat, a flower-bordered flight of apartment stairs, or simply a brightly painted front door. No matter how small or large your home's entrance, it can still call out a hearty welcome. Your porch may grace a standard mid-town brownstone or a grand Queen Anne wrap-around, but the important thing is that it is *your* front porch, the place where you welcome others into your life.

The porches in my life have been important threads in my family tapestry. They were where the greetings and partings of family and friends took place. Our times on the porch bound us together, and I imagine that my family used our front porch in a rather old-fashioned manner, transforming it into an outdoor living room as people used to do before the days of television and air conditioners. I cherish my childhood days of playing games on the porch, spending delicious hours napping and daydreaming, and looking forward to the warm companionship of a friend who was as welcome as the

> *Friendship is largely dependent upon porches.*
>
> DOROTHY SCARBOROUGH

summer's breeze. Today, many people use modern conveniences such as air conditioners, televisions, and computers—especially during the hot summer months—and seem to spend most of their at-home time indoors. But I love spending my summers—and every other season of the year—the old-fashioned way. I prefer the charm of the front porch.

Growing up in the South, we passed countless hours on our porches. In good weather, we could pass nearly all day on our front porch, treating it as an extension of our living room. Grandparents chatted and reminisced while we children nibbled on homemade treats. Depending on the season, daffodils and tulips bloomed in porchside planters, fireflies in mason jar lanterns brought flickering light to the evening, brilliant red and orange leaves floated from trees to ground, snow drifted quietly down to blanket the front yard, and the changing year's joy lasted from sunup to sundown every day.

How about your porch—or your stoop, or your front door? Is the path to your door brimming with cheerfulness? Does your porch give a favorable picture of the people who live in the home? Whether decorated with simple clay flowerpots planted with pansies and a cheery front door wreath, or comfortable wicker chairs and casual ticking-stripe cushions, or even elaborately detailed furnishings and ornate landscaping, the image on the porch should whisper a word of welcome long before you answer the knock at the door. Your porch doesn't have to be perfectly arranged or expensively furnished. After all, you don't even need a porch at all! But the entrance to the place you call home does require some planning and creativity, for it speaks volumes about who lives just beyond the door.

Nobody thought much about the front porch when most Americans had them and used them. The great American front porch was just there, open and sociable, an unassigned part of the house that belonged to everyone and no one, a place for family and friends to pass the time.

DAVIDA ROCHLIN

Over the years I've collected stories and ideas about making the front porch special. While the old adage about fences making good neighbors is probably true, I prefer to think that porches make good friends. You can tailor these suggestions to fit the personality of your own home. For instance, if you don't have an actual front porch but love the idea of dining outdoors in good weather, try setting up a simple set of table and chairs, or even spread a cozy blanket, in the front yard. For it is the spirit of front porch hospitality, not the porch itself, that makes all the difference.

Season by season, I invite and welcome you to my front porch.

Sandy Lynam Clough

Spring

CELEBRATING NEW BEGINNINGS ON THE FRONT PORCH

When the first tender buds of the spring peep through their snowy blanket, I begin fluffing the pillows on my front porch, readying it for the season to come. Amid my preparations, I notice that a little jenny wren has built a nest in my Boston fern as she has done for the past few springs. I like to believe that it is the same little wren that keeps returning to rebuild her nest and sit on my porch spring after spring. And every year I receive the blessing of watching her little fledglings graduate from a safe and secure nest, first to a limb not far away, then eventually off to see the far-away world.

As the miracle of spring unfolds, I like to think of my front porch as a cozy nest in which family and friends find the reassurance and courage to make a fresh start, fulfill a long-awaited dream, take up an interesting new hobby, or simply make good on a promise to a friend.

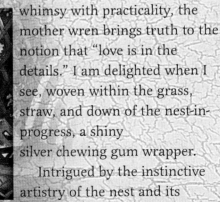

Seated comfortably among the pillows on my front porch, I watch the little jenny wren gloriously weave her nest so small. Despite its unassuming size, it is a nest perfectly furnished with all the necessary creature comforts of a little bird family. Blending whimsy with practicality, the mother wren brings truth to the notion that "love is in the details." I am delighted when I see, woven within the grass, straw, and down of the nest-in-progress, a shiny silver chewing gum wrapper.

Intrigued by the instinctive artistry of the nest and its maker, I pointed out the mother wren to my husband and two sons. Soon they were equally fascinated with the wren and her activities, and we spent many an hour sitting on the porch, watching as the little Boston fern household took shape and the cozy, downy abode underwent preparations to become a family nest.

> *Fancy a porch in the early morning, when the flowers have fresh-washed faces, when the dust is laid by the dew, when the happy stir of life goes on all about.*
>
> DOROTHY SCARBOROUGH

As the world burst into bloom with delicate crocus, sunny daffodils, and jewel-colored tulips, the story in the nest continued as tiny dappled eggs miraculously hatched. Basking in the pleasure of the bright spring day, my family and I watched from the porch as the mother wren worked ever so hard to nourish her four fledglings with woodland confections of spiders and insects steeped in the morning dew.

The little birds had the world at their feet and were anxious to begin their exploration, but we couldn't help but wish that they would remain in the nest just a little longer. One day, lured by the sweetness of wisteria and sunshine, the young wrens took to limb. We watched our small friends with pride, thankful for the insights of nature they had granted us. We smiled and exclaimed as one by one they hopped from nest to fern, then from fern to nearby wisteria limb.

Whenever I think of the little wrens taking flight, I am reminded of the springtime beginnings and transitions that have taken place in my own family—my two sons graduating to the next year's class in school; a springtime picnic that marks both the birthing of a new season as well as a time of getting reacquainted with old friends; the digging of new garden plots and planting of never-before-tried flower and vegetable seeds. Springtime brings a world of things to hope for and look forward to. Amid an end-of-the-school-year picture-taking session on the front porch, I pause to find joy in the moment, savoring it and recording it on the treasured film of memory. When I look back at my front porch pictures, I see myself and my loved ones growing and changing, readying ourselves for each new goal and challenge to come.

Springtime family gatherings on the front porch, complete with long hours of planning and dreaming, inspire us to find happiness in the present and to build anticipation for the future. Just as the little jenny wren builds her nest anticipating the arrival of a new generation, family and friends can gather on the front porch to witness the arrival of the season of new beginnings. For the front porch is the best place to sit to view the changing world, and the world just outside that first front porch step is full of wonder and new adventures. Safe and secure in our porch world, rooted and steeped in family love and tradition, we plan our next steps out of the nest, onto that limb, off to see the world, knowing in our hearts that we can return time and again to the welcoming comfort of the front porch.

READYING THE PORCH

• As butterflies wing off to the sun and birds feather their nests with nature's building materials, I find myself inspired to do a little spring cleaning on the front porch. Tackle the job from the eaves to the floor and a sparkling porch will be yours to enjoy for the entire season. I love to give the floor of my porch a fresh coat of paint early in the spring. Later on in the summer, it will feel smooth and cool to bare feet. Pesky spider webs seem to pop up on the porch overnight. To clean the corners where they linger, brisk away their calling cards with an unused paintbrush. A dry, clean paintbrush is one of my favorite housekeeping tools because its bristles easily fit into the corners of rocking chairs and the slats of the porch swing. A good polish of lemon oil will instantly renew and refresh the finish of wood furniture. Vacuum your wicker often, especially during springtime, to keep pollen from sticking. If you don't have a front porch, freshen up your front door with a colorful, high-gloss coat of paint to complement your home's exterior hue!

DECORATING FOR THE SEASON

• Just because a bowl, cup, or saucer is chipped doesn't mean you have to toss it away. Simply move it out to the porch, where it can be transformed into a plant saucer, iced tea coaster, or even an artistic display on an easel. Try turning a chipped teacup on its side, resting it on its saucer. Inside the teacup place a miniature bird's nest filled with tiny eggs for a cheery springtime display.

Porchside Gardener

• My gardening friend Demi taught me how to "age" new clay flowerpots. In a mixing bowl, add a handful of moss (fun to find on a woodland stroll) to two cups of buttermilk. Crush the moss to release its spores into the buttermilk. Dampen the clay pots with water and "paint" them with the moss and buttermilk mixture. Seal the pots in plastic bags. In just two weeks, your clay pots will sport a wonderful antique green tint.

• Even the most inexperienced gardeners can cultivate ivy. This wonderful vine can easily be grown in a secluded corner of the yard or in a flowerpot that winters over nicely. Hardy ivy will grow in sun or shade. Ivy stays green all year long and looks lush as a part of any party table setting. Because ivy grows and spreads very quickly and can easily take over a garden plot, be sure to keep it in its place!

• Ivy planted just a few days ahead of a springtime

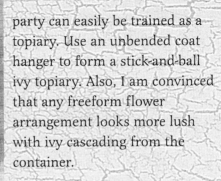

Along the front of the porch scarlet sage is standing, in bright independence, with dusty miller as a foil. All day long the humming birds are poising to sip the sweetness from those honeyed tiny pitchers, their whirring wings making monotonous harmony and their little quivering cries stabbing the silence.

Dorothy Scarborough

party can easily be trained as a topiary. Use an unbended coat hanger to form a stick-and-ball ivy topiary. Also, I am convinced that any freeform flower arrangement looks more lush with ivy cascading from the container.

A Well-Lit Porch

• As the spring days gradually begin to linger longer, pay careful attention to the lighting on your front porch. Tiny white lights extend easily beyond the Christmas season. String them along a trellis or weave them through a cascading rosebush. On my front porch I have trained wisteria to twine along the edge of the eaves, and one Christmas I put the tiny white lights through the branches. My mother suggested I leave the lights up all year long so when the wisteria blooms and then leafs out, lights and vine will be intertwined. I use an electric timer to switch the tiny lights on for a few hours in the early evening, and now I enjoy magical, romantic lighting all year long.

PORCHSIDE GETAWAY

• Whether entertaining friends or spending quiet time alone, a quick little spring getaway may be closer than you think—right outside on the front porch! Welcome springtime and its pleasures by decorating the porch with an eye toward pleasing all of the senses. Add a soft, pastel quilt that feels smooth to the touch during a blissful afternoon nap. Plant a lilac tree near the front porch. It will bloom by Mother's Day and will look as lovely as a fresh, hand-picked bouquet. Its fragrance will linger in the spring air, especially when skirts brush by and release the delicious aroma of lilacs. Keep a wide-brimmed straw hat casually tossed over the corner of a chair ready to accompany you on a spontaneous spring stroll through the azaleas as you take in their heady scent. Listen carefully for the chirps of birds returning from winter's chill. Keep buttery shortbread, fresh fruit, and refreshing raspberry tea on hand for a quick but satisfying porchside afternoon tea. Delight in the season as the slow rhythm of the creaking front porch rockers gently eases your cares away and renews your soul.

NATURE ON THE PORCH

• For a creative and whimsical decorating accessory, save empty bird's nests and display a collection of them on the front porch. A carefree array of feathers adds to the theme. The nests also look cute with real-looking eggs placed in their center. If you are lucky, you might find half of a pretty blue robin's egg to display. Birdhouses are also fun to collect, especially from travels as they come in so many styles. Cluster a variety of them in a corner of the porch for a welcoming outdoorsy touch.

• Hang a pretty hummingbird feeder from the eaves of the porch. Attract the birds by planting a nearby flower bed with bee balm and red salvia. You can easily make your own hummingbird

Sandy Lynam Clough

nectar for the feeder by mixing one part sugar with four parts water. Dissolve the sugar in boiling water. It is not necessary to color the solution once the hummingbirds have discovered your feeder. If the ants discover it too, simply grease the string you hang the feeder on with butter to prevent them from climbing up into it.

PROJECTS FOR THE PORCH

Mismatched teacups and saucers provide inspiration for many porchside decorating projects:

- Fill teacups with water and float votive candles in them for a festive spring luncheon place setting.
- Plant herbs in teacups and share their fragrant bounty with a neighbor.
- Use saucers as iced tea coasters. Arrange sprigs of mint next to the glasses.
- Carefully hot glue miniature teacups to a grapevine wreath to

> *It is not the variegated colors, the cheerful sounds, and the warm breezes which enliven us so much in spring; it is the quiet prophetic spirit of endless hope, a presentiment of many happy days, the anticipation of higher everlasting blossoms and fruits, and the secret sympathy with the world that is developing itself.*
>
> MARTIN OPITZ

> *He who refreshes others will himself be refreshed.*
>
> THE BOOK OF PROVERBS

form a welcoming door decoration.

- African violets planted in teacups look charming and also make everlasting party favors.
- Remember—three or more teacups make a collection!

THE OUTDOOR TABLE

• A round table draped with a timeworn quilt and topped with a coordinating vintage square tablecloth makes dinner on the porch a special occasion. I like to complete this cozy yet elegant table setting with lighting from my collection of hurricane lamps. I make sure to keep oil in my lamps at all times, for they are also wonderful—and functional—when the electricity goes out during a spring thunderstorm. Some of my hurricane lamps were rescued from tag sales, some are family heirlooms, and one is extra special to me because a very thoughtful friend carried it safely to me in her suitcase all the way from Connecticut to Arkansas!

• For a festive spring centerpiece, plant winter wheat grass seeds in a clay flowerpot. Water the soil faithfully and the seeds will quickly grow. Add decorated pastel eggs and tie a bright ribbon around the pot for an inexpensive yet beautiful arrangement. If you didn't plan ahead to plant the wheat grass, you can always count on ivy for a versatile decorating accessory. A vintage birdcage filled with a six-inch pot of ivy cascading out its open door and tied with a beautiful ribbon makes a wonderful last-minute centerpiece.

• Use a six-inch piece of ivy to create charming napkin rings. Simply tie the ivy in and around the napkins. Use cloth napkins, as they are reusable and look more elegant than paper. These festive napkin rings look especially pretty displayed on a pastel tablecloth that is topped with Battenburg lace.

• Pin a pretty bow and ivy cuttings to the corners of a square tablecloth. Encircle the edge of a round table with a long piece of freshly washed ivy, pinning every so often as needed to secure it to the table. A ten-inch grapevine wreath woven with ivy makes the freshest charger plate.

• Petite bird's nests make festive springtime place settings and party favors. In the palm of your hand, mold sphagnum moss in the shape of a bird's nest and let it dry as formed. (A little hairspray helps it hold its form.) It's cute to set the moss nest on a small twig and place two or three foil-wrapped chocolate eggs in each nest. Put a nest beside each place setting with the guest's name written on a small slip of paper.

PORCH PURSUITS

• The herb rosemary, which symbolizes remembrance, reminds me to keep a basket filled with pretty notecards and favorite pens for writing inspiring (and perhaps overdue) thank-you notes. It's fun to tie several sprigs of rosemary to the handle of the basket with a ribbon. Sometimes I even break a fresh piece off my rosemary plant and enclose it along with the note as a fragrant surprise to the recipient.

• A large woven basket with a handle can store all of those mail-order catalogs that you only dream of having enough time to browse through. This spring, be sure to make time on a nice afternoon to pour yourself a glass of lemonade, put up your feet, and engage in several uninterrupted hours of catalog shopping on the front porch. No crowds, no parking hassles—just you and the fragrant outdoors!

A PLACE FOR FRIENDSHIP

• May Day is a traditional time for celebrating good friends and neighbors. Renew a favorite custom of anonymously leaving flowers tied to your neighbor's front doorknob. A bouquet of blossoms arranged in an old-fashioned cobalt blue medicine bottle does the trick. Tie a paper doily nosegay-style around the bottle. Add a bow with extra ribbon, leaving enough to tie onto the doorknob. No matter what your age, have fun ringing the doorbell and running!

CHILDREN ON THE PORCH

• An abundance of flowers on the front porch is a necessity for grownups and children alike come springtime. Create colorful, overflowing, fragrant planters that celebrate childhood with a playful hand and a festive touch. Consider using inventive, whimsical containers such as a little red wagon with spring annuals cascading down its sides. In one corner of my porch sits my son's now-outgrown bright yellow dump truck. It brings back many wonderful memories and looks so cheerful filled with sunny impatiens that liven it up in its new place of honor.

> *Fair Spring! whose simplest promise more delights*
> *Than all their largest wealth, and through the heart*
> *Each joy and new-born hope*
> *With softest influence breathes.*
>
> ANNA LETITIA BARBAULD

A Springtime Luncheon on the Front Porch

Asparagus Roll-ups
Shoepeg Corn Salad
Ham with Pineapple Glaze
Flowerpot Cheesecakes
Lemonade

ASPARAGUS ROLL-UPS

This is an easy do-ahead-of time dish. Prepare and place cookie sheet in refrigerator with clear plastic wrap. Place under the broiler when needed. If I use this as an hors d'oeuvre, I cut the roll-ups in half. Just before serving, I squeeze the juice of a lemon wedge ever so lightly over each roll-up. It adds zing!

16-ounce can asparagus spears, drained
6 slices sandwich bread, crust trimmed off
1/4 cup melted butter
1/4 cup pecans, chopped
1/2 teaspoon seasoned salt

With pastry brush, brush bread slice with melted butter and place two spears of asparagus on each slice of bread. Sprinkle with seasoned salt and 1 teaspoon chopped pecans. Roll up and secure with a toothpick. Brush top again with melted butter and sprinkle with Parmesan cheese. Place on a cookie sheet under broiler 3-5 minutes until golden toasty brown. Serves six.

SHOEPEG CORN SALAD

16-ounce can shoepeg corn
16-ounce can French-style green beans
16-ounce can small green peas
2-ounce jar chopped pimento
1 cup celery, chopped
1 cup green pepper, finely chopped
1/2 cup onion, chopped
3/4 cup sugar
1/4 cup salad oil
1/2 cup vinegar

Drain canned vegetables. Mix canned vegetables with fresh vegetables in a 2-quart bowl with a lid that seals tightly. To prepare dressing, heat sugar, oil, and vinegar together in pan on stove. Cool dressing mixture and pour over vegetables. Refrigerate overnight to allow flavors to fully mix. This salad keeps for many days in the fridge and improves with age. Makes 12 1/2-cup servings.

Note: Shoepeg corn salad is especially good for gatherings on the porch that linger long into the afternoon or evening because it does not contain mayonnaise and will not easily spoil.

PINEAPPLE GLAZE FOR HAM

Mix 1/2 cup brown sugar, 1/4 teaspoon ground cloves, 1/2 cup crushed pineapple, and 2 teaspoons prepared mustard. Spread over baked ham about one hour before end of cooking time.

FLOWERPOT CHEESECAKES

8 new 3-inch terra cotta flowerpots
8 vanilla wafers
instant cheesecake mix
crushed Oreo cookies
plastic drinking straws
fresh seasonal flowers

Run eight new 3-inch terra cotta clay flowerpots through the hottest cycle in the dishwasher. When clean, place a vanilla wafer in the bottom of each flowerpot. Next, pour instant cheesecake mixture into each pot (Jell-o cheesecake mix works well), leaving approximately 1/4 inch of room at the top. Place a drinking straw in the center of each "cheesecake," and cut the straw off even with the top of the flowerpot. Sprinkle the surface with crushed Oreo cookie crumbs to form the "dirt." Refrigerate until cheesecake is set. Just before serving, place a fresh flower through the center of the straw. I like to use jonquils, grape hyacinths, or even roses. Place all flowerpot cheesecakes together on a pretty serving tray. They make wonderful table centerpieces as well as yummy desserts!

LEMONADE

Always a welcome springtime treat, lemonade may be freshly squeezed or quickly made from a powdered mix. Serve it in a five-gallon pickling crock covered with a clean, fresh tea towel. Before serving, add crushed ice, a strawberry or two in each glass, and garnish with a sprig of mint. An antique enamel ladle adds a fun, old-fashioned touch.

And all the woods are alive

with the murmur and sound of spring,

And the rosebud breaks into pink on the climbing briar,

And the crocus bed is a

quivering moon of fire

Girdled round with the belt

of an amethyst ring.

OSCAR WILDE

Summer

FLAGS AND FAMILIES ON THE FRONT PORCH

For many decades now, my father has flown an American flag from the front porch of his home. When I was a child, the flag was one of the first signs of summer's arrival. And now, just like my father, I fly a flag from my front porch every summer, for flags and front porches have special meaning to my family and me. They celebrate the freedom of summer, a time to laugh and play and spend long hours in the company of those we love best.

A flag accompanied my mother as she stood on the steps of my grandmother's porch over half a century ago as a young bride. She bravely kissed her new husband good-bye and watched him ride off on a bus, knowing that his eventual destination was the Second World War.

Many months and prayers later, my father was ever so fortunate to return home and walk up those same porch steps to join his new wife on a blessed journey through life together. Through all of the trials and tribulations of war, Daddy came safely home to a flag flying proudly on the front porch and a loving wife waiting to embrace him.

After the war ended, Daddy returned to the tools of his trade—a saw, a hammer, and a tape measure. A skilled carpenter in the midst of a postwar building boom, Daddy's talents were very much in demand. Every day at five o'clock, I can recall him coming home with his olive green metal lunch box in hand, climbing the porch steps as we scampered out to greet him.

Daddy was still working hard as a carpenter when I was in Mrs. Porter's sixth grade class and came home with a tough homework project—writing an essay about "What the American Flag Means to Me." At the time, it was one of the hardest assignments I'd ever encountered. That night, while my mother washed and dried the supper dishes, I pondered the topic, then decided to seek valuable help from Daddy, who was sure to have an opinion on the subject.

Sure enough, Daddy was delighted to share with me what the American flag meant to him. He told me that the flag meant "not having to go where anyone tells you to go, or having the freedom to say whatever you want to say, or being free to do whatever you want to do." Then Daddy explained why he flew the American flag from the front porch in the summertime: "It was the freedom of coming home from the war. That is why I fly the American flag on our porch, for all the world to see that we don't ever take for granted the freedoms with which we are blessed."

Most of us have never had to be the ones to fight for the freedoms we sometimes take for granted. But we do give thanks for those freedoms, especially during the cheery days of summer when family gathers together and the flag waves gently in the breeze from its post on the front porch.

I listen closely now as I hear my sons recite the Pledge of Allegiance in their school flag ceremony. As their mother, my prayer is that, when they are grown, they will come freely home from work every day carrying their lunch box or briefcase. May they live well and laugh long and love much. It is with appreciation for family and freedom that I proudly fly my flag every summer day, cherishing those I love best and the memories, values, and traditions that have drawn us so tightly together. Summer on the front porch—flag flying, children playing, family sharing—is truly something for which to give thanks.

READYING THE PORCH

• For a refreshingly shaded porch in the heat of summer, tie several strings that reach from the ground to the top of the porch, spacing them evenly apart. Plant morning glory seeds in the ground by the strings and watch the plants climb up toward the summer sun. A wooden clothespin holds the young plants in place and gets them started on the correct string. My mother planted morning glories this way every summer. One year she mixed up her seeds and mistakenly planted green beans instead of morning glories. We all had a good laugh, and we certainly enjoyed eating the fresh beans off the vine.

• Come summer, nothing welcomes front porch visitors quite as well as bright bouquets of flowers. An old-fashioned watering can resting on the porch steps and brimming with zinnias adds a welcoming note to your entire home. If you don't have your own garden, travel along a country road and gather an armful of wildflowers or visit a fresh flower stand. To make summer flowers last longer, I add approximately six drops of bleach and a teaspoon of sugar to every quart of water in the container or vase. Change your display as the weeks and months pass—phlox and delphinium in June, zinnias and snapdragons in July, Shasta daisies and sunflowers in August.

DECORATING FOR THE SEASON

• My daddy has long since retired from his trade as a carpenter, but his toolbox has kept on working. It sits proudly on my sister's front porch as the perfect planter for bright red geraniums. You too can decorate your summer porch with meaningful items or collections—seashells spotted on a summer vacation at the beach, colorful leaves gathered on a woodland stroll, feathers found on a family nature walk, heirloom lamps and lanterns handed down from great aunts and grandmothers. These make wonderful, conversation-starting seasonal displays for your front porch.

PORCHSIDE GARDENER

• By July the hydrangea blossoms are as big as cabbages and the scent of gardenias perfumes the air. When planning the summer garden, remember to include especially fragrant flowers such as four o'clocks, sweet peas, and moonflowers, and a variety of herbs such as thyme, basil, and lemon balm. Their fragrance will linger in the late afternoon and evening stillness.

• Peppermint, spearmint, lemon mint—plant a mint near the porch so you can easily pluck a leaf when filling a glass of iced tea or lemonade. Potted mint is easy to grow and so fragrant. If you want your plant to thrive and branch out, pinch off the top leaves and give them away to a friend. Mints and other herbs look cute planted in chipped teapots and teacups. Rosemary and basil are fragrant cooking herbs that grow best when they are regularly pinched back. Rosemary looks especially pretty in a porch planter, formed into a topiary. When you divide your mints, plant some in teacups to share with your neighbors.

• A summer tradition in my garden is planting geraniums on the sunny side of the porch and impatiens in the shade. Ferns add a cozy touch, and birds love to call them home. Pass an idle hour on the porch poring through a stack of favorite gardening magazines and seed catalogs.

• Use imaginative vases to display cut flowers. Pretty tag-sale bottles, old-fashioned pottery crocks, and mason jars are some of my favorites. I keep mason jars on hand for so many occasions, including large parties that require many floral displays. Tie a pretty ribbon around the jar's rim and add a handful of flowers to create an instant centerpiece. Try displaying flowers in antique teapots and teacups, glasses and goblets. Sometimes the smallest containers can make the biggest impression!

A Well-Lit Porch

• As the evening hours of summer fade into darkness, cast a warm candlelit glow on the porch that encourages guests to linger long after the meal is finished. Floating candles are especially refreshing in the summer's heat. Fill shallow bowls with water, then float votives and even fragrant gardenia blossoms in them.

• Mason jars make wonderful hurricane globes for column candles and also prevent the night breeze from blowing the flame out. Support the tall candles with an inch or so of sand at the bottom of each jar. Miniature clay flowerpots serve as cute votive holders too. You can also use cracked or mismatched teacups as votive cups. Add four tablespoons of water to the teacup to prevent the wax from sticking to the sides and to allow the votive to be easily replaced.

Porchside Getaways

• Whether entertaining friends or spending quiet time alone, pull up a rocking chair and a soft, timeworn quilt. If you are lucky enough to have a porch swing, keep it filled with pillows patterned in summery prints like cabbage rose chintzes. Antique tablecloths add cottage charm and softness to a side table. Write in your journal, sketch the summer scenery, or take a well-deserved nap in the soothing atmosphere of your luxurious outdoor room.

Seated with Stuart and Brent Tarleton in the cool shade of the porch of Tara, her father's plantation,...she made a pretty picture. On either side of her, the twins lounged easily in their chairs, laughing and squinting at the sunlight through tall mint-garnished glasses as they laughed and talked....

Margaret Mitchell
Gone With the Wind

• Spend quiet time on the porch watching a summer rainstorm quench the lawn. Remember to take in the fresh smell of the rain as you ponder the season's beauty.

NATURE ON THE PORCH

• Choirs of crickets and tree frogs begin to sing as the night falls. Sit outside late one night and enjoy their summer serenade.

• Here in the South, fireflies in summertime are as abundant as the stars in the sky. Drift off to sleep surrounded by their magical light by placing several fireflies in a mason jar with holes punched in the lid. (Make the holes small enough so they can't escape in the house!) Let them fly away the next morning after enjoying their sparkles for a memorable night.

PROJECTS FOR THE PORCH

Mason jars have countless creative uses...
• For a neighborhood gathering or a family reunion, fill mason jars with homemade iced tea. Garnish with fresh slices of lemon and sprigs of peppermint.
• A ribbon bow tied around the neck of a mason jar filled with a bouquet of flowers makes a fresh summer table centerpiece.

> *Yes, there will be an abundance of flowers and singing and joy!*
>
> THE BOOK OF ISAIAH

- Mason jars serve as inexpensive yet cute hurricane lamps when they contain lit votives.
- Kids love to watch tadpoles hatch in a mason jar home.

• Along with a flag flapping in the breeze, ease into summer with the melodic sound of wind chimes on the front porch. You can easily make your own set of silver chimes. You will need: six utensils of mismatched silverware, one of which must be a fork; a hammer; needle-nose pliers; a drill; and a fishing line. Using the pliers, bend out the prongs on the fork and curl the ends upward. Next, flatten the other utensils by wrapping a towel around them and carefully pounding them with the hammer. Drill a hole in all six handles. Hang one flatware utensil from each prong of the fork with fishing line, and hang one utensil in the center of the chime for balance. Next, tie some fishing line in the "hanger" fork. Put your creation to the breeze and enjoy its music.

THE OUTDOOR TABLE

• Every summer, my mother purchased bushels of corn, purple hull peas, and green beans from the local farmer's market. We spent our afternoons

> *The porch is the true center of the home, around which life flows on gently and graciously, with an open reserve, a charming candor. One does not stay inside the house more than is absolutely necessary, for all such pleasant occupations as eating and sleeping, reading, studying, working, and entertaining one's friends are carried on on some companionable piazza or other.*
>
> DOROTHY SCARBOROUGH

> *Mother and Father were sitting... with a group of friends. They were no doubt rocking away in the big rockers that furnished the porch, talking about the bridge hands they had held that evening, and enjoying the view of the moonlit valley below Cumberland Mountain.*
>
> PETER TAYLOR

shelling and shucking the vegetables, getting them ready for freezing and canning. Sunday dinner was true to tradition as we ate Southern fried chicken with a bounty of garden-fresh vegetables—fried okra, sliced tomatoes, snappy green beans, sliced cucumbers, and crisp green onions. Homemade cornbread slathered with honey and butter melted in our mouths, and somehow we always made room for lemon icebox pie or strawberry short-cake.

• If you are lucky enough to still have your child's little red wagon, you can fill it with ice to chill canned drinks in a fun and decorative manner. The red wagon cooler is especially popular at summertime parties and reunions, and kids will enjoy pulling it around and offering refreshments to the adults!

PORCH PURSUITS

• The front porch is a wonderful place for singing, playing, and listening to music. If possible, hold your music lessons on the front porch. Violin lessons held on our porch and taught by a visiting

instructor help keep our children's interest level up—and the practicing to continue—during the summer months. The outdoor music room keeps things unique and creates a stage-like atmosphere. Later in the evening, children can give their own performances for family members.

• An antique mailbox standing in the garden makes an ever-so-convenient storage spot for gardening gloves, clippers, twine, scissors, and favorite hand tools. You can also store pencils and sketchpads, toys and games, and other craft supplies inside the mailbox if you don't have a garden.

KIDS ON THE PORCH

• Making clover chains is a fun activity for young guests. A lap full of fresh-picked clover stems laced together can create an array of summer necklaces, rings, and bracelets.

• Keep a collection of brightly colored water guns in a creative container on the front porch. A water gun fight provides lots of laughter and fun when sun and spirits are high. Listen for the bells of the ice cream truck, for creamsicles and fudgesicles provide the perfect con-clusion to a water fight.

• Sing silly songs in the front porch swing, for the most beautiful sound of all is the sound of laughter.

Pass on songs from your childhood such as "Do Your Ears Hang Low?" "Row Row Row Your Boat," or "On Top of Old Smoky." Giggles will soon erupt and hugs are sure to follow. Laughter is a favorite sound of summer.

All green and fair the Summer lies,

Just budded from the bud of Spring,

With tender blue of wistful skies,

And winds which softly sing.

SUSAN COOLIDGE

Summertime Supper on the Porch

Fourth of July Grilled Hamburgers
Aunt Hattie's Baked Beans
Dallas Dip
Porch Potato Salad
Easy Lemon Icebox Pie
Watermelon
Tea Punch

AUNT HATTIE'S BAKED BEANS

My Aunt Hattie was famous for her baked beans. Every family reunion, we looked forward to eating her traditional recipe.

4 slices bacon, chopped
1 large yellow onion, finely chopped
2 16-ounce cans pork and beans
1 tablespoon prepared mustard
1/4 cup chile sauce

Cook bacon in iron skillet until crisp. Remove bacon, add chopped onions, and cook until onions are clear. Remove onions from bacon drippings and mix with bacon, pork and beans, mustard, and chile sauce. Brush a 1 1/2-quart casserole dish with bacon drippings. Pour bean mixture into casserole. Bake uncovered at 350 degrees approximately 45 minutes, or until beans are brown and bubbly. Makes eight servings.

DALLAS DIP

This dip is the perfect accompaniment to a sandwich or burger supper. Make it the night before, for it tastes better if the flavors are able to blend in the fridge overnight. Refrigerated, it keeps for several days. I make this dip every summer as it is a most-requested recipe and easy to prepare for a large crowd.

6 large ripe tomatoes, diced and chopped
12 green onions, thinly sliced
2 cans green chiles
2 large cucumbers, peeled, diced, and chopped
2 tablespoons garlic salt
1/4 cup apple cider vinegar
2 tablespoons olive oil

Combine all ingredients. Let chill in refrigerator overnight. Serve with tortilla chips.

PORCH POTATO SALAD

The secret to this salad is that it contains very little mayonnaise. Its creamy texture comes from sour cream. Keep this refreshing potato salad on ice in the heat of the summer. It is a wonderful make-ahead dish to bring to a family reunion or to enjoy as part of a summer supper on the porch.

8 medium potatoes
1 cup celery, finely chopped
1/2 cup sweet pickle relish
1/2 cup small radishes, thinly sliced
1 large onion, finely chopped
1/2 cup sour cream
3/4 cup mayonnaise
1 teaspoon celery seed
1 tablespoon mustard
1/2 teaspoon garlic salt

1 1/2 teaspoons table salt
2 hard-cooked eggs

Cover potatoes with water and boil 20-30 minutes until they are fork-tender. Drain and cool. Peel and cut potatoes into 1/2-inch cubes. Combine potatoes, celery, pickle relish, radish, and onion. Mix gently with a wooden spoon and set aside. Combine sour cream, mayonnaise, celery seed, mustard, and salts. Pour over potato mix and stir lightly. Slice hard-cooked eggs on top as garnish. Cover and refrigerate several hours before serving to allow flavors to blend. Serve eight to ten.

EASY LEMON ICEBOX PIE

2 prepared 10-inch graham cracker crusts
1 quart vanilla ice cream, softened
1 small can frozen lemonade concentrate
Fold together ice cream and lemonade concentrate. Pour mixture into pie shells and dust with a few cracker crumbs for garnish. Put back in freezer until hardened enough to slice. Garnish each piece with a thin slice of lemon, a fresh strawberry, and a mint leaf.

WATERMELON

Arkansas is known all over the country for its sweet, prize-winning watermelons. Putting on country airs, the men and children have never outgrown the need for a seed spittin' contest!

TEA PUNCH

1 gallon iced tea
2 cans frozen five-flavor punch
2 cans water

Mix iced tea with fruit punch. Add water. Serve in mason jars with crushed ice, mint garnishes, and miniature American flags. Easy to make and very festive!

The porches here are covered in vines of various sorts, that make a bowered privacy in places, yet leave a clear view of the hill and the lake and the road. There are rose vines along the columns, Marechal Niels with their golden loveliness, and climbing American beauties, that a little earlier were a mass of delight, and white climbers, and pink ones. On a back porch an old-fashioned yellow rose of humble origin is allowed to clamber, with its unassuming flowers and its faint odor.

DOROTHY SCARBOROUGH

Sandy Lynam Clough

Autumn

GATHERING TOGETHER ON THE FRONT PORCH

I'm grateful that most Southern families make it a priority to get together. Sometimes gatherings among relatives just happen, but once a year you can always count on the big family reunion. My family is no exception and, as my father was one of ten children, ours is quite a gathering. So many nieces, cousins, aunts, and uncles showed up at a recent reunion that the front porch of a favorite cousin's home wouldn't hold all of us for the traditional family portrait. Some relatives had to spill out into the azalea bed in front of the porch!

My family holds our reunion every September, and I have only missed three gatherings in my lifetime. When I was a young girl, the reunion was always held at my grandparents' house in the country. As we traveled down a winding, dusty gravel road, the rooftop of the house would slowly emerge and soon I would see an army of cars parked in the open yard. Battered work trucks stood next to brand-new Cadillacs, and our green Studebaker would join right in. As we made our way up toward the house, we were greeted with generous hugs and arms outstretched to help us carry the many dishes Mother had spent the previous day preparing.

While the women busied themselves putting the final touches on what was to be a grand meal and the men engaged in lively discussion out on the porch, we children created our own entertainment. As a city child, I found it wonderful to scamper through the pasture, free of a fenced-in yard. In the lower part of the field, my cousins and I discovered a corn crib filled with corncobs. I don't remember who threw the first corncob, but soon we'd drawn up sides—girls against boys. Corncobs flew as we held up garbage-can-lid shields. Laughter rang in the hills until two of my cousins suddenly started screaming at the top of their lungs. In the midst of our fun, we had unknowingly stirred up a wasp nest, and now the wasps had joined the battle. Breathlessly we all ran back to the house to assess the damage. My aunt rubbed match heads on our stings to ease the pain, and our tears quickly dried as homemade peach ice cream was quickly brought out.

While we children ate lunch, mothers chatted with us as if to catch a glimpse of the future in our words and expressions. Perhaps they could imagine my cousin Zack graduating at the top of his class and becoming a neurosurgeon. After all, it was Zack who rushed us back to the house and saved us from further wasp stings that day. Perhaps they correctly guessed that we would be blessed with many teachers in the family, as well as a politician, a bronco-bustin' rider, a banker, and several farmers.

It seems that a new baby had arrived every year, and we were always grateful for the reunions when

> *May our house always be too small to hold all our friends.*
> MYRTLE REED

everybody could make it back. Today, memories for future generations are in the making as my own family returns year after year to the annual gathering. This past reunion was particularly emotional for me, for my eighty-six-year-old daddy attended the reunion without my mother by his side. Through the tears and hugs, I knew this was where we needed to be on that day—among the family that has loved each other for so many years. When we gathered on the front porch for the annual family portrait, I knew that the place my mother held will always be in our hearts, for in her usual spot a new baby was held in its mother's arms.

In the spirit of the old hymn "We Gather Together," the harvest we give thanks for is a precious one. The bounty we celebrate is that of our loved ones safely gathering from the often harried and stressful world around us. The gentle spirit of front porch living is a welcome gathering of family homecomings where we can lay aside business and count our blessings of abundance.

When I was growing up, the front porch days of autumn were among my happiest. I always looked forward to the yearly family reunion, candlelight dinners on the porch in the crisp air, curling up in the porch swing with an enthralling book, and celebrating friendships with a mug of hot cider, fresh slices of pecan pie, and good conversation. Autumn is a time to join hands with those we love as we call our families to the table. It is a time to count our blessings.

The season of autumn also encourages us to return home in our hearts as the wind whistles a reminder that winter is just around the corner. One of my oft-repeated prayers is that my two sons will keep our home forever in their hearts. May we hold dear in our hearts forever the family members and friends that mean so much as we welcome the brisk days of autumn to the front porch.

READYING THE PORCH

• If you are hosting a large gathering, you need not fret about rounding up extra chairs. For fun places to sit on the porch or lawn, use hay bales, which are certainly most appropriate for the season. Toss fall-patterned tablecloths over them and they become quite cozy. After the party, you can use the hay as mulch for flowerbeds and gardens to protect perennial plants from winter's chill. You can also use hay bales to build an artistic seasonal display by adding

pots of chrysanthemums, pumpkins, and gourds of all shapes and sizes and a homemade scarecrow by the front door as the official greeter of autumn.

• Savor the smells of fall—spicy, warm apple cider, the first wood-burning fire of the season, the crisp autumn air. For a simple yet delicious fragrance on the front porch, sprinkle cinnamon *inside* the jack o' lantern.

The lands are lit
With all the autumn blaze of Golden Rod;
And everywhere the Purple Asters nod
And bend and wave and flit.

HELEN HUNT

God looks down well pleased to mark
In earth's dusk each rosy spark,
Lights of home and lights of love,
And the child the heart thereof.

KATHERINE TYNAN

• Whatever your home's style, whatever your decor, porch furnishings that can take the weather as it changes and provide carefree comfort work the best. Make the most of your own front porch as an outdoor living room with individual touches that make it your own. Keep cozy wool blankets in muted colors and toasty sweaters nearby on the porch swing for nippy autumn evenings. Candles, books, and mugs of hot cider are traditional fall favorites.

SEASONAL DECORATIVE TOUCHES

• A trip to the local farmer's market on a crisp October day provides you with an abundance of the season's best offerings. Pumpkins, gourds, and Indian corn all make festive decorations. Pumpkins come in so many sizes, from the small, petite pumpkins to the large jack o' lanterns. The unusual color of white pumpkins adds interest to the display. Gourds also come in many shapes, sizes, and colors. Choose several ears of Indian corn in varied colors and tie them together with raffia to make an easy door or table decoration. A basket filled with a variety of these treasures on the front porch steps announces to your guests that cheery autumn has arrived.

PORCHSIDE GARDENER

• Gather on the porch on a crisp October evening to relax in a rocking chair and view the glorious display of autumn colors. If a view from the porch includes an object that is an eyesore, you can plant nasturtiums, honeysuckle, or annual morning glory. Install a lattice trellis and let the fragrant vines climb and cover it. You don't need to have a big decorating budget—God took care of that already.

A WELL-LIT PORCH

• With the days growing shorter but still with plenty to do, good front porch lighting becomes more of a necessity. Apples and small pumpkins make charming holders for votive candles. With a sharp knife, cut a candle-sized hole in the top of the apple or pumpkin. These lanterns from nature look especially charming surrounded by brightly colored fall leaves.

PORCHSIDE GETAWAYS

• Things for an autumn afternoon getaway on the front porch: a steaming mug of cappucino or Russian tea; flannel quilts in earthy fall colors; sweet and crunchy apples; a lacy white cloth and fresh flowers on a side table; an antique letter opener for lingering

over the day's mail; a magnifying glass for closer inspection of a butterfly; a stack of classics to immerse yourself in. Stay late to watch the harvest moon rise!

Nature on the Porch

• A gathering of nature's treasures on the front porch is sure to put a smile on the faces of those who visit. Gather gifts of autumn on woodland walks and collect lichen-trimmed branches, mounds of moss, chunks of tree bark, and pine cones in a large basket. My favorite fall floral arrangement is colorful leaves, branches, and berries mounted on twigs. The herbs rosemary, lamb's ear, and lavender add to the fragrant smell of fall. Grapes tucked into and cascading out the sides of a flower arrangement done up with velvety red cockscomb show off autumn's rich earthy tones.

• Listen to the sounds of fall on the front porch— hoot owls, nightingales, howling wind, crunching

leaves underfoot, school bells. Hear the laughter of children returning home from school, and the giggles of kids and pets playing in newly raked leaf piles.

PROJECTS FOR THE PORCH

• Grow autumn gourds next to a nearby fence and use them to make your own birdhouses. Carefully cut a two-inch hole in the gourd and scrape out the inside with a spoon. Let the gourd dry for about two weeks, then spray it with a clear acrylic sealer. (This protection allows it to last longer.) My gourd birdhouses have lasted for several years already!

• Make a cheery homemade scarecrow to welcome autumn guests to your front porch. You will need:

old flannel shirt
pair of old blue jeans
pair of old boots
straw hat
36-inch piece of rope

6-foot wooden tomato stake
3-foot wooden tomato stake
heavy twine
pair of cotton gardening
    gloves
needle and thread
medium-sized pumpkin
plenty of straw

Fashion the wooden stakes into a cross, binding them securely together with heavy twine. Make sure you leave at least 12 inches in length sticking up above where they meet.

Using sturdy doubled thread, sew the ankles of the blue jeans and the cuffs of the sleeves shut. Stuff the jeans tightly with straw all the way up to the waist. Attach the flannel shirt to the jeans by tucking it in and stitching it together all the way around. Place the end of each sleeve into a straw-filled cotton glove and sew it all the way around. Insert the wooden stake all the way through the scarecrow's unbuttoned shirt, down through one of the pant legs, and out the bottom so

Yellow, mellow, ripened days,
Sheltered in a golden coating;
O'er the dreamy listless haze,
White and dainty cloudlets floating;
Winking at the blushing trees,
And the sombre, furrowed fallow;
Smiling at the airy ease
Of the southward flying swallow.
Sweet and smiling are thy ways,
Beauteous, golden Autumn days.

WILL CARLETON

Those who plan good have joy.

THE BOOK OF PROVERBS

it extends about 12 inches past the bottom of the pant leg. This will allow you to stake the scarecrow into the ground.

Put the shirt sleeves through the arm stake, and stuff the shirt so it is quite full, buttoning up as you go. Thread rope through the belt loops to fashion a belt.

To create the head of the scarecrow, secure the pumpkin in place on top of the stake so it comes to the neck of the flannel shirt. For a finishing touch, attach the straw hat to the pumpkin head with long straight pins to keep the wind from blowing it off. When you have placed Mr. Scarecrow where you want him, put the pant leg ends into the boots. I usually prop one leg bended on a bale of hay. You can also add pots of chrysanthemums and extra pumpkins to the autumn display.

At our annual fall party, I leave a space next to the scarecrow for a popular picture-taking spot. With the hay, pumpkins, and mums—and, of course, Mr. Scarecrow—it's a memory for the making.

I save my scarecrow from year to year, adding a little more straw each season as it settles. It doesn't matter if Mr. Scarecrow gets wet; he dries out just fine in the sun.

THE OUTDOOR TABLE

• Tables laden with fall fruits and vegetables invite both nibbling and conversation. Chili served in a chunky mug and thick slices of pecan pie are perennial autumn favorites. Warm apple cider both tastes yummy and warms chilly hands. Serve it in a blue enamel tin cup for a homespun touch.

• For an easy-to-make yet striking centerpiece, place jelly jars filled with water and flowers in a small pumpkin. A mason jar filled with water in a larger pumpkin makes a bigger centerpiece. Add seasonal fall wildflowers to make it extra festive. Yellow flowers such as chrysanthemums displayed with red, orange, and gold leaves make a beautiful fall arrangement. Place a fresh or dried flower arrangement in an old-fashioned watering can and set it on the porch steps.

PORCH PURSUITS

• Fall is a winding-down season, but there is still a whirlwind of activity with leaves to rake, brisk walks to take, apples to pick, next spring's bulbs to plant, and pecans to gather. Reward the day's accomplishments by treating yourself to a slice of warm pumpkin bread and a cold glass of apple cider out on the front porch.

• Autumn is a prelude to Christmas, the busiest holiday time of the year. Around Thanksgiving, school children usually have a short break in their schedule, college students return on their first long weekend at home, and working adults get to savor several days of vacation. To keep home in our hearts for

As I lie restfully on this quiet porch, I watch the days swing by, recorded in this calendared garden before me. …I know not which is more beautiful, the June riot of roses and of daisy-snowed fields, the loveliness of Queen Anne's lace in midsummer, or the Midas miracle of goldenrod in autumn.

DOROTHY SCARBOROUGH

family members or good friends, the autumn front porch gathering need not be lavish to be rich in memories. Sometimes simple times together provide the best memories—telling stories while munching on crunchy apples.

KIDS ON THE PORCH

• The back-to-school sweater days of autumn can be celebrated by creating a cozy ambience on the front porch that keeps memories alive for parents and children alike. Starting on the very first day my sons went off to kindergarten, I have taken pictures of them standing in the same spot on the front porch wearing new school clothes and holding lunch boxes and backpacks. This picture-taking session has become an autumn ritual in our family, and we always decorate the porch for the season to mark the special occasion.

Menu for an Autumn Afternoon on the Porch

Easy Chili with Assorted Toppings
Best-Ever Spinach Dip in a Pumpkin Bowl
Toasted Pumpkin Seeds
Pumpkin Bread
Pecan Pie
Hot Mulled Cider

EASY CHILI WITH ASSORTED TOPPINGS

1 pound ground beef
1 tablespoon butter
1 medium onion, chopped
1 2-pound can Mexican-style beans
1 can cream of tomato soup
1 can rotel tomatoes
1 teaspoon salt
1 tablespoon chili powder
shredded cheddar cheese
chopped green onions
corn chips

Brown beef in skillet with butter and onion. Add beans, soup, tomatoes, salt, and chili powder. Simmer one hour. Top with cheddar cheese, green onions, and corn chips. For a larger gathering, or perhaps for unexpected guests, extend the use of this recipe by spooning it over cooked macaroni. As my mother used to say, "There's always room for one more person."

BEST-EVER SPINACH DIP IN A PUMPKIN BOWL

1 10-ounce package chopped frozen spinach
1 can water chestnuts
2 cups sour cream
3 tablespoons mayonnaise
1 package dry Knorr's vegetable soup mix
3 green onions
dip-sized corn chips

Thaw and drain spinach. Drain water chestnuts and chop coarsely. Mix all (except corn chips) ingredients and spoon into a medium-sized, cleaned-out pumpkin. Serve with corn chips. Set pumpkin bowl inside a rustic twig wreath. Add colorful fall leaves around the base and you have the centerpiece too!

TOASTED PUMPKIN SEEDS

Before preparing this recipe, save out a few uncooked pumpkin seeds. Children will enjoy planting them next spring. The seeds will keep nicely through winter in a dry envelope.

2 cups pumpkin seeds
1 tablespoon vegetable oil
1/2 teaspoon salt
1/4 teaspoon garlic

Rinse off pumpkin seeds and pat dry with paper towels. Toss seeds with oil and spread them out on a cookie sheet. Bake at 350 degrees for 20 minutes, tossing them every 5-7 minutes, until golden brown. Remove from oven and pour into paper grocery bag.

Add salt to bag. Hold top tightly closed and shake to salt evenly. You might want to make a double batch of these for take-home party favors. Simply fill clean, dry baby food jars with seeds. Cut out a six-inch circle of fabric and tie it with a raffia bow around the lid. Place jars in a straw-filled basket on the front porch step so guests won't forget to take home their festive gifts.

The sunbeams dropped
Their gold, and passing in porch and niche,
Softened to shadows, silvery, pale, and dim,
As if the very Day paused and grew Eve.

EDWIN ARNOLD

PUMPKIN BREAD

3 1/2 cups all-purpose flour, sifted before measuring
2 teaspoons soda
1 1/2 teaspoons salt
2 teaspoons cinnamon
2 teaspoons nutmeg
3 cups sugar
4 eggs, beaten
2/3 cup water
1 cup salad oil
2 cups (1 16-ounce can) pumpkin
1 cup pecans, chopped

Combine flour, soda, salt, cinnamon, nutmeg, and sugar in large mixing bowl. Add eggs, water, oil, and pumpkin. Stir until blended. Add nuts and mix well. Butter and flour three 1-pound empty coffee cans. Pour mixture into cans, dividing evenly three ways. Bake at 350 degrees for one hour. Cool cakes slightly in cans and turn out on rack to finish cooling. This is best made the day before it's needed. It is especially pretty because of its round slices. Eat one loaf with friends, put one loaf in the freezer, and tie a pretty ribbon around another loaf and give it to a friend or neighbor.

PECAN PIE

This recipe is a favorite of mine. It comes from my mother, who was quite well-known for her pecan pies. I usually double the recipe—one for company and one for the freezer that comes in handy for an impromptu gathering. It freezes very well.

3 eggs, beaten
2/3 cup sugar
1/3 teaspoon salt
1/3 cup melted butter
1 cup maple-flavored pancake syrup
1 unbaked 9-inch pie shell
1 cup pecan halves

Combine eggs, sugar, salt, butter, and pancake syrup in a medium-sized bowl and mix well. Pour mixture into pie shell and top with pecan halves. Bake at 375 degrees for 45 minutes.

HOT MULLED CIDER

1 gallon apple cider
1 cup orange juice
1/2 cup red hot cinnamon candies
4 three-inch cinnamon sticks, broken
1/2 teaspoon ground nutmeg

Prepare cider using a large automatic coffee maker. Substitute the cider for the water. Place the rest of the ingredients in the coffee basket and brew. Serve hot in tin or enamel mugs topped with orange slices. The fragrant aroma of this cider is sure to keep everyone gathered on the front porch!

A porch has a hospitable soul. It welcomes guests of all degrees in a more cordial manner than the inside of a house ever knows. A porch comes halfway to meet a guest, with outstretched hands, and bids him a lingering good-by when he must go.

DOROTHY SCARBOROUGH

49

Winter

TIMES OF REFLECTION ON THE FRONT PORCH

In celebration of the first snowfall of winter, I step out onto my front porch to view the magical glitter of the newly white world. Just beyond the porch stands a stately old oak tree. It is believed that this mighty tree was merely an acorn, just establishing its roots, during the Civil War era. The sculpture of the winter tree, its outstretched limbs festooned with snow, looks magnificent against the darkness of the night sky. Tall and stately amid the landscape, this living symbol conjures up images of strength, endurance, hope, and promise. I reflect upon the promise that branches now bare will burst forth into bloom again, budding into a splendid cloak of regal green.

Along with the snowfall and dreams of spring to come, winter brings the best reason to celebrate of all the seasons—the joy of Christmas. During the bustling holidays, we eagerly await friends, family, and those we love making the traditional journey home. With all of the shopping, wrapping, baking, and decorating, Christmas is the time of year when we must promise ourselves to pause and celebrate the joy of family and friends. Sometimes in the mad rush of things, it is so easy for us to unwittingly break our promises. "I promise, we'll see you next time," we earnestly tell a friend. "I promise I'll take you to the toy store, but right now I'm just too busy," we say to a small child. Yet in the quiet and still of winter, God never breaks His miraculous promise, and next spring the buds burst forth into bloom.

While it's important to spend time with others

during the holiday season, we must also take advantage of the quiet of a front porch winter morning or evening for ourselves. In the midst of the holiday hustle and bustle, quiet time on the porch gives us moments to reflect, give thanks to God, and be still. Winter on the front porch is an ideal time to engage in spiritual moments of solitude and reflect upon our lives. And we are rewarded with peace, renewed to go back inside and give of ourselves to others.

In appreciation of winter, I linger on my front porch watching the snow fall. I look forward to the energetic celebrations of the coming winter days, whether it is hosting a porch full of carolers, organizing a sledding party, or watching a New Year's Eve fireworks display. I welcome friends both old and new to my front porch. I cherish the hugs and fulfilled promises of family members.

The trees sparkling like diamonds shine brightly in the stillness as I watch my breath drift by in the winter chill. As each snowflake quietly falls, I am reminded of the story of a man named Wilson Bentley who, using his big bellows camera, discovered that no two snowflakes were alike. As holiday traditions bring family and

What is pleasanter than the tie of host and guest?

RALPH WALDO EMERSON

friends together, I ponder what makes each one of us so special. After all, like the snowflakes, no two of us are alike; we are all unique.

Winter on the porch is a time of reflection and quiet, looking back and looking ahead, forming new goals and dreaming new dreams, examining ourselves and the part we play in the world around us. In winter, time-honored promises and traditions are passed on from one generation to the next, strengthening our family ties and enriching our lives. Even if a return home for the holidays is only in our hearts and wishes, we are comforted by the promise that God's love never fails and that He forever welcomes us with outstretched arms.

I think perhaps of all the seasons on the porch, winter is my favorite. Remember, the size of your porch—or, for that matter, your stoop or front door—need not be grand in scale to be charming. Its only requirement is that it conveys a hearty spirit of welcome before the doorbell is even rung. The first snowfall of the year is a perfect reason to make a big pot of hearty homemade vegetable soup and invite the neighbors over for dinner and board games. The sled being pulled from storage instantly calls children to gather round. Sitting on the front porch as part of the audience of winter fun I watch the joy of winter in action as a family builds snowman after snowman, young children draw up sides for a snowball fight, and yet more little ones giggle as they make snow angels about the yard. As the days of winter chill set in and another year comes to an end, the warmth of family and friendships shines through the beauty of all the seasons on my front porch.

> *The conversation that human beings carry on would be sincerer, gentler, kindlier, if it were uttered on open porches with the peace of pine trees and whispering waters and candid sky about.*
>
> DOROTHY SCARBOROUGH

ornaments; a friendly snowman family dressed in scarves and galoshes, waving hello from the lawn; red and green tartan plaid blankets and pillows cozily arranged in the porch swing. Remember to keep the season's warmest wishes at heart, and your home will convey the message of hospitality and welcome each day of winter.

• A gracious entry begins on the front porch. To bear your message, paint a sign over the door in acrylics that carries an inspiring message such as, "Love and Joy Come to You."

• Prepare the front porch with the greenery of Christmas—magnolia, pine, boxwood, juniper, fir, holly, cedar, ivy, and, to bring the bounty of winter's harvest to the season's table, green apples and pears too!

• "Don we now our gay apparel..." The words of this favorite carol can also be applied to our porches. Glad tidings and merriment are that much nicer among the holly boughs and frosted window panes.

READYING THE PORCH

• A porch that says "welcome" brightens up dark winter months. To create an entryway that greets guests throughout the holiday season and beyond, pay attention to the special touches—a tree on the front porch decorated with homespun, rustic

DECORATING FOR THE SEASON

• Cozy up your winter days on the front porch by changing your fabrics to match the season. In woodland camp style, cover chairs with plaid woolly throws or blankets. The colors of forest green and holly berry red will take you through the holiday season and brighten up gray afternoons in January and February. Decorate your porch in casual country style that is as fresh as nature and makes the outdoors feel as warm as indoors by the fire.

There were a good deal of laughing and kissing and explaining, in the simple, loving fashion which makes these home festivals so pleasant at the time, so sweet to remember long afterward.

LOUISA MAY ALCOTT
Little Women

PORCHSIDE GARDENER

• For an aura of natural extravagance, use quantities of greenery and ribbon on the front porch. "Plant" an array of holiday greens—pine, holly, cedar, fir, and juniper—in your front porch urns and flowerpots. They won't grow or take root, but they will create a delicious smelling display of lush winter greenery. My sister got carried away with this idea when she moved into her brand-new house. Very little landscaping had been done at that point, so she went into the woods and dug up four-foot-tall cedar trees to "plant" around the corners of her porch. Her children decorated them with white twinkling lights, and the trees looked as if they were growing! You'll be surprised how long your outdoor arrangements will last in winter's cold. Some last right into spring!

• Though winter winds may rattle window boxes, they can still be outfitted in seasonal finery. Fill window boxes with greens secured in the dirt, which serves as a holding medium similar to florist foam. Transform windowsills into stunning Christmas scenes with an abundance of apples, swags of spruce, and armloads of fresh holly.

A WELL-LIT PORCH

• As the most celebrated of all the year's holidays draws near, friends and family welcome each other in from the cold to share in the joys of the season. Our front porches are symbols of welcome, showing open hearts and outstretched arms. My favorite memory from my visit to the heart of Pennsylvania's Amish country was that of the light in the window. Simple candles glowing in each window served as warm beacons to those approaching the household. When darkness falls early in the evening, you too can fill your porch with candlelight like the Amish.

I heard the bells on Christmas day
The old familiar carols play,
And wild and sweet,
The words repeat
of peace on earth,
good-will to men.

HENRY WADSWORTH LONGFELLOW

55

Many miles away from Pennsylvania, I have adopted the tradition of displaying a single candle in the window of my Southern home, for the warm light of hospitality is in style anywhere.

• Create a path of brilliant luminaries to welcome parties of carolers to the front porch. You will need:

> votive candles (one for each bag, however many you plan to make)
> brown paper lunch-size bags
> sand

Under the snowdrifts
the blossoms are sleeping,
Dreaming their dreams
of sunshine and June,
Down in the hush of their quiet
they're keeping
Trills from the throstle's wild
summer-sung tune.

HARRIET PRESCOTT SPOFFORD

• Decorate a table on the porch with a traditional train set or a sprawling Christmas village. Or you can simply set a winter evening aglow with a collection of candles that vary in size, shape, and scent. A candlelight tablescape on the front porch greets your visitors with light and fragrance.

PORCHSIDE GETAWAYS

• Engage in a refreshing moment of solitude on the front porch and watch the lights of winter—starlight, candlelight, Christmas lights, moonlight, luminaries, and lanterns.

Open the top of the brown bag. Fold down the top of the bag to make a one-to-two-inch cuff at the top. (This will help keep the bag open.) Pour approximately one cup of sand into the bottom of each bag, then place a votive securely in the center of the sand. Line your porch steps or driveway with the bags, light the votives, and enjoy the festive illumination for several hours.

• Bring a toasty cup of cocoa out to the front porch and listen to the quiet of winter—the creak of snow-laden branches; the soft dripping of icicles; the sound of animals padding across the snowy yard. Or simply be still and take in the quiet.

• Celebrate the joy of the season by tuning your ears to hear the bells of winter—doorbells, jingle bells, sleigh bells, church bells. Bells provide a chorus of

good cheer at this special time of hope, love, and laughter. Bells, bells, bells pealing out over the church steeples herald the arrival of the holiday season, the time of year filled with activities and traditions that bring family and friends together.

Nature on the Porch

• Baskets layered with evergreen boughs and filled with herbs, reindeer moss, and rosehips add to winter's abundance of apples, pine cones, berries, and ivy. Generous use of these plentiful materials makes for classic Christmas arrangements and bespeaks volumes of grace and charm.

• Winter is yet another season to delight in feeding the birds. After our family has enjoyed our indoor Christmas tree, we "plant" it outside and redecorate it with food for the birds, such as pine cones rolled in peanut butter and birdseed. I also save bread crumbs and cereal leftovers with the bird tree in mind. Not a crumb goes to waste! Put your tree in a place where you can watch from your window the activity of birds and squirrels enjoying their own Christmas tree. A bird feeder near the porch that is easy to refill on winter's coldest of days brings a gift of plenty to God's small creatures. After the birds and squirrels are through eating the treats off their secondhand tree, my sons and I take the tree down to the pond, where it takes on yet another role—that of a new home for fish that will spawn in the spring.

PROJECTS FOR THE PORCH

• Holly and ivy, pine and cedar—nature's standbys for Christmas are easily brought to the front porch. Take a trip to the woods to cut fragrant boughs, branches, and vines. Carry a large bushel basket and return home with it brimming full. The boughs can be easily paired with decorating materials already on hand. For instance, a bough of greenery tied around a lamppost with a big red velvet ribbon is a simple but luxurious touch in the spirit of holiday welcome.

• I enjoy using snowmen as a decorating theme for Christmas. They are the perfect friends to carry you through all the Christmas holidays and on into winter's chill. For a winter party, I use foamcore to make life-sized Mr. Snowman and Mrs. Snowman characters. Magic markers make easy the task of drawing the jolly snow people, and I use an Exacto knife to cut out a round circle for their faces. I place the snowmen leaning up against a chair on the porch, and the neighborhood children (as well as an adult or two!) love to peer their faces through. It's generally our most popular Kodak picture spot of the season.

• Birds are always grateful for a yummy winter treat. To make it, you'll need:

> 2 cups saved bacon drippings or suet
> 1 cup sunflower seeds
> 1 cup wild birdseed mix

Melt bacon drippings or suet in a saucepan and stir in all the seeds. Spoon into hollowed-out orange halves and place in a muffin tin to keep upright. Cool in refrigerator until solid. Hang treats from a branch with a twine handle. If you have any leftover suet-seed mixture, you can use a spatula to "ice" a pine cone with cooled suet and seeds. Hang it on a limb and enjoy watching the mealtime activity. To make Christmas even more festive for feathered friends, hang a tiny wreath above the birdhouse door.

THE OUTDOOR TABLE

• Enjoy a taste of winter on the front porch—a white enamel dishpan full of buttery popcorn to munch on while you watch the sledding; mugs of hot cocoa with melting marshmallows to warm little bodies that have made a village of snow angels in the front yard; "remarkable" fudge on a red-and-green plate served in appreciation to front porch carolers; fresh-baked sugar cookies especially for Dad to say "thank you" for putting up the Christmas lights. And don't forget the freshly made snow ice cream!

PORCH PURSUITS

• When the holidays are over for the year and spring is just around the corner, one of February's little luxuries is curling up in a cozy wool blanket on the porch swing with a basket brimming with all the new seed catalogs. In planning next year's garden, a view from the porch gives you a good overall picture of what part of your garden is in the shade and what part is in the sun. Of course, you will need to take into consideration that the trees will leaf out and create further shade, and that the sun will move higher in the sky as spring arrives. Consider planting native species or flowers that will attract bees, butterflies, and hummingbirds to your garden. Perhaps begin a perennial garden for year-after-year color, or learn creative uses for treasured herbs. You can also plan to create a formal rose garden in a sunny spot. To start one you need just a single rosebush, but let that one bush be magnificent. Study and reflect ways the garden can make your life richer, your days more beautiful, and your blessings more bountiful. In winter's quiet and still on the front porch rocker, plan to make your life more special.

KIDS ON THE PORCH

• Even if your children are grown, you can still put to use their winter mittens—as a decorating accessory! A basket on the porch filled with colorful mittens always awaited my young boys as they headed out to play in the snow. Once they were instructed to put both mittens back in the basket after playtime, we cut down on mismatched mittens! Now that my sons are older, their mittens from boyhood look cute hanging on a grapevine wreath or strung on a garland of greens along the porch rail secured with wooden clothespins.

• In the spirit of winter fun and wishes of snowfall, lean a sled up against the porch wall. It will be ready and waiting just when the kids need it!

A Taste of Winter on the Porch

Sledding Popcorn
"Remarkable" Fudge
Fresh-Baked Sugar Cookies
Snow Ice Cream
Toasty Cocoa

SLEDDING POPCORN

Place a heated bread warmer in the bottom of a white enamel dishpan (the kind with the red rim around the top). Generously heap with popped popcorn and sprinkle with Parmesan cheese for a boost of sledding energy. It is so inviting to have a dishpan full of popcorn for everyone to grab a heaping handful!

"REMARKABLE" FUDGE

I like this recipe because it is the favorite—yet easiest-to-make!—recipe that my family used to make. Little ones love to help prepare the Christmas fudge.

4 cups sugar
1 12-ounce can evaporated milk
1 stick (1/2 cup) butter
1 12-ounce package semi-sweet chocolate chips
1 teaspoon vanilla
1 7-ounce jar marshmallow cream
1 cup pecans or walnuts, chopped

Cook sugar, milk, and butter in a heavy pan for nine minutes, stirring frequently to prevent mixture from sticking. Remove from heat. Add chocolate chips, vanilla, marshmallow cream, and nuts. Beat until chocolate chips are melted and blended. Pour into a buttered 13 x 9 x 2 pan. Cool and cut into squares. Makes 9 dozen one-inch squares. We always said it was called "remarkable" fudge because it's gone before you know it!

FRESH-BAKED SUGAR COOKIES

These cookies served warm will reward Santa's helpers who string the brilliant lights of Christmas on the roof of the porch and decorate the house with holiday cheer.

1 1/4 cups all-purposed flour, sifted before
*   measuring*
1/4 teaspoon baking powder
1/4 teaspoon salt
1/2 cup shortening
3/4 cup sugar
1 egg
1 tablespoon milk
1 teaspoon vanilla

Sift together flour, baking powder, and salt. Cream shortening, add sugar gradually, and cream shortening and sugar together until light and fluffy. Beat in egg, then mix in milk and vanilla. Stir in the dry ingredients. Chill dough. When dough is chilled, roll it very thin and cut with cookie cutters into desired shapes. Place cookies on a lightly buttered baking sheet and sprinkle with sugar. Bake at 425 degrees for 5-7 minutes, watching carefully to make sure that they don't burn. Makes five dozen cookies. These cookies are easy for children to help with, especially in cutting out the shapes of stars, trees, and ornaments. To make colored sugar, put granulated sugar in a sealable bowl. Add 1-2 drops of red or green food coloring. Seal lid tightly and shake vigorously for Christmas-colored sugar.

SNOW ICE CREAM

One of my favorite growing-up memories was that of Mother making snow ice cream on the front porch for all the neighborhood kids. When she started to make the ice cream, children seemed to magically appear. One thing that's important to remember— gather fresh, clean snow! Don't dig too deeply, and gather your snow from an area that is out in the open, away from any bushes or trees.

1 large bowl of snow (approximately one quart)
1 cup heavy cream
sugar, to taste
1/2 teaspoon vanilla

Beat the heavy cream, then fold in sugar and vanilla. Take a large bowl outside and scoop up the snow while it is still frozen. Fold cream mixture into snow. Adjust the sugar and vanilla to taste, and your winter treat is ready to eat on the front porch. Have plenty of spoons on hand, for there's sure to be many tasters! Watching fireworks in the winter evening while eating a bowl of snow ice cream is surely a memory in the making.

I crown thee king of intimate delights,
Fireside enjoyments, home-born happiness,
And all the comforts that the lowly roof
Of undisturb'd retirement, and the hours
Of long, uninterrupted evening, knows.

COWPER

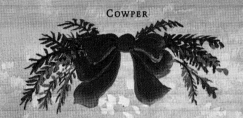

May the spirit of giving
Go on through the year,
Bringing love, laughter,
Hope, and good cheer.
Gifts wrapped with charity,
Joy, peace, and grace,
Ribboned with happiness,
A tender embrace.

NORMA WOODBRIDGE